A Thousand Horses Out To Sea

MONGREL EMPIRE PRESS
NORMAN, OKLAHOMA, UNITED STATES OF AMERICA

2016

FIRST EDITION, 2016

A Thousand Horses Out To Sea
© 2016 by Erika T. Wurth

ISBN 978-0-9972517-3-9

Cover Art
"Fire Woman Pray" illustration
© 2016 by Douglas Miles

MONGREL EMPIRE PRESS
NORMAN, OK

ONLINE CATALOGUE: WWW.MONGRELEMPIRE.ORG

This publisher is a proud member of

COUNCIL OF LITERARY MAGAZINES & PRESSES
w w w . c l m p . o r g

Book Design: Mongrel Empire Press using iWork Pages

A Thousand Horses Out To Sea

Erika T. Wurth

CONTENTS

THAT SMALL WOODEN BOX

-For Mark Wedeven, talking shop with S & C now.

GOD IN THE WEST

*You don't know what love is but you know how to raise it
in me like a dead girl winched up from a river.*

~Kim Addonizio

Leaving the Glow

There are fireflies here,
and at sunset, they come out.
I think of my white cousins in New York,
how we chased them with jars
capturing them so that we could watch them float,
and glow under our hands.

We were greedy and beautiful and even ideal,
our white hands and Indian hands praying the same way,
to the same light, our family watching from the dusty grey porch,
before everyone went off into their separate adulthoods,
leaving the glow of the evening far behind.

Dusty Redemption

These streets, these days are a mirror, walking down Central,
my face and their faces the same, the neon lights on 66 making us beautiful.
Asleep on concrete slabs, eyes closed, black eyelashes trembling,
waiting for the bus, you know the one, the one that never comes.

Like children in this Albuquerque sun, passed out,
dirty but made clean in this familiar light.

I walk across the street in a mean dream,
pushing the big, black walk button, the pole covered in stickers,
waiting for a sign, something to flash, white light in the shape of a man.

This dusty redemption, this weird heat making everyone angelic,
pushing our skin outward, inward, inside out,
we're becoming something else,
something that our mothers never expected,
something they had to learn how to love
with eyes closed, their arms folded widely over ours;
like a butterfly that had been hovering above, and finally, out of exhaustion,
lay down on the strange red flower that it thought it had known below.

Distant as a Planet

My house smells like an old hotel room and feels like an old hotel and you are as distant to me as a planet, but somehow when I look up I can see it—my wound, my original wound gone now and soaring up above me harsh and beautiful as any star. Bright, lyrical, your long brown hands reach for me from this distance and it feels like when you would touch me in our own bed. Hot, strange and shining brightly, I could burn under your hand, and then, when I was nothing, a crisp black star of paper, I could float up to you, trapped on that cold blue mountain forever now, and dream.

He Brought Me Down

He brought me down on the old grey carpet
in the empty room, the smell of smoke and blood
everywhere, the girl he didn't want
waiting outside.

In that empty room, the darkness
complete, my head racing with images of her face,
how it mirrored mine with her long dark hair
in her long black car, in the middle of the desert,
her eyes narrowing into mine, his short dark hands rough
but walking in beauty and on the edge,

I came to understand what those hands wanted of me.

He said he couldn't help himself
his mother a teacher, his father a medicine man,
my long yellow body like so many others
wrapped around his small one,

his skin the darkest cedar.

Days later, on that last night under the stars
I don't know if we woke the neighbors,
but something dark and dangerous came awake inside me,
sliding back into the grass, a blooming of something bright
as the blood that had come from my hand that first night,
when I'd gone to open the bottle of cheap white wine
for the girl he was going to put aside for me only hours later.

You're strong, she said.
Yes, I said, pushing down and watching the blood rush forth.

Curled in Their Shirts

It's 4:30 am. That's the time I always wake
to look at the clock and sigh,
remembering the words that came to me
in a dream, or the man who came
in a nightmare, and left, just as quickly
as the words I'm trying so hard to grasp.

I'm lucky though. Mainly the words
that I'm looking for stay and the men go.

But both wake me, curled in their shirts,
all coming to the same end.

Flat black signs on a page
that can only last for so long,
before we all curl back
into that final sleep, that final poem.

Fists Clenched, Holding

In the Anodyne, in the middle of this wild red city of wind and dust,
she would slide her hands over the old green pool tables, over
the new brown arms of the boys next to her, their sticks
hitting the mark, her hands in her pockets, her money in her fists.

And she would tell me about her man, the one she said she loved,
though I was never quite sure, his children with many billygannas,
women he'd met here, their hands in their pockets, their fists clenched too.

How he would go back to them or to others like them, after their storms.
After the rain had flooded the streets, the monsoon had passed,
I'd say leave him; my voice as useless as stones dropped
in the deepest part of a well, and forgotten.

Beasts at Her Feet

She liked the beasts at her feet best, the ones with their heads so
large and brown and full of black black hair she could sink her
teeth into them and hold hard and fast at her breast and beat back
back back beast back before you can eat her not that she won't let
you because she's hungry for the hungriest ones the ones who
can't control themselves whose paws beat at her legs begging to be
let up to curl up up and around her and take her back to the wild
white heat from which she'd come.

Sweet Brown Violins

She was a gangster in Greeley a girl from Cali
don't fuck with me don't fuck with me,
        she'd sing, her eyes Aztec and naked
        their headdresses long and green and shimmering
        letting you know
I'll cut you—
baby baby I love you I love you
his fingers like sweet brown violins on her skin and she would arc like the music
with her eyes closed, trembling until the huehuetl ended
and his fingers had only begun their demands.

GOD in the West

In Tucson, in the bar where a man who calls himself GOD will brand his name on you for five dollars, from the entrance you can see the steam rising, and the newly religious yelling for GOD in the West, the poets at the bar waiting for something to transform them, their hands on their glasses, on the wood, in their own Indian hair, religion in the girl running back and forth across the room yelling for GOD and for Pabst Blue Ribbon, in the shot that one of the poets bought the other, in the woman watching the girl getting branded for life, telling her to brand her own name and the girl rolling her eyes and saying *I like GOD and I like Pabst Blue Ribbon*, in the clouds moving quietly in the dark outside above the heads of the unknowing poets, in the iron that presses to the flesh, the flash of enlightenment after as the camera's pulled up, and in the girl who simply sits down from where she had been standing above and like a tiny new god, admires her newest wound, consecrating all of the others, and then looks up, asking for her free shot and takes it, her blue eyes glowing with the kind of knowledge only the very strange and very beautiful ever fully understand.

Faces Towards the Light

During the day, holding their grandmother's soft, dusty hands,
faces turned to the light

Native American Church boys, Santa Maria boys;
candles holding the light in their faces,
fingers still burning from the match

on these streets the mad, rolling black trucks
pumping noise into air, their cigarettes lit and ready, their voices feral

I walk downtown, under the bridge;
broken bottles, souls rising up, wandering

Change Form Behind Me

Light a candle for me, since I cannot smoke this cigarette,
because I'm out of cigarettes, and don't smoke anyway, not tonight.

Light one for the Virgin de Guadalupe, because my grandmother loved her,
her sweet brown hands praying in the light, to the East, to her own cigarettes.
She started smoking when she was only a child amongst criminals,
abandoned, enlightened, full of shadows only she would keep.

Light a cigarette for me in the dark, outside the bar,
so that I can shiver for you and for the cold,
trying to figure out which one I fear most.

Light the way down the road, so I can watch the shadows follow me in the
night, the things that change form behind me, the magical animals making their
magical noises and my magical heart going dark in the dark in the dark.

Your Eyes to the Sun

Don't worry, you'll find your reason to drink.
Someone will break your heart hard and clean and like a bone that needs to be
re-set, you will fix it like a maniac doctor with all of the wrong things,
a maddened expression on your romantic Indian face, because you are both
the doctor and the patient, waiting to be clean, waiting to set sail, drinks
on the Riviera, drugs in Mexico, you will have it all, you will pass out
like the rest of them, beautiful and bright and shining as the day you were born,
your eyes on the sun, no burn, your back to the sand, until you sink.
And find your reason to drink.

Ghosts Floating on the Flat White Bed

They say there's a ghost in the bathroom here. I've passed her many times, waiting to hear her cry. That's what she does, cry in the bathroom, like any girl. Like the girls in the bathroom at the Jr. High dance. Like my mother after my father's pale hand would strike her. She only cries for men, someone said.

Outside her prison doors, I wait for those that force this ocean, for the Indian angel I cannot be, for the girl who lives in the bathroom crying for a man that is long dead.

This is where the most intimate truths occur; ghosts floating on the flat white bed where the words or the hands dance, where the children cry, regardless of their ages, when the things that we say destroy each other.

Around My Neck

It's been a phoenix, an angel, a woman with drooping breasts, a dove, something I hold in the dark while I pray to my grandmother, the child I don't hold in my arms, the gun she held in hers, the bottle in his, the thing, the final thing I touch before I sleep, waiting for my prayers to be lifted up, over me, floating back to wherever they came from.

The Column High

You were like the moon you gave yourself, strange and obsessed,
your hair grey, your eyes as dark as the darkest river at night,
light reflecting on the water, never moving beneath.

When you laughed, it was only out of bitterness

you're young you're young you'd chant *you'll see*
and I wondered if you meant the beauty and the blood—
the heart of things.

But you were cruel, and born of dust,
in a place where Indian and Spanish went round and round.
Still you spin, the column high, your eyes open, your arms embracing the wind.

On North Beach

On North Beach with Leon de Leon
I told you how I'd been pointing with my lips
and my hand. How Indian your eyes were
and Leon, pointing with his lips, looked like a cousin—
you laughed and crushed your paw into that great mass of black curls.

You'd called me from a pay phone, and we'd wandered, dancing,
until you called again, forgetting, I put your name in my phone, later
I called from Castro letting it ring again and again until it said it was
disconnected.

In the taxi, hours before, I had imagined calling that number,
your hand on the other end reaching for the blackness of the phone,
and quickly disappearing, the bum who'd sang to me earlier for a dime,
picking up and telling me how I made him feel so brand new.

I Call My Sister Instead

I've become the one who calls in the middle of the night,
though I've never called anyone in the middle of the night, Indian
or white, telling him I loved him and listening to her turn in the bed.
Instead, I sit at home in my own bed, turning, listening to my back ache.
One more drink will make it better, I call my sister instead.
She sighs and turns in the bed. I ask her why
don't they bring their girlfriends, and the baby cries,
and she has to hang up and I look at the ceiling,
at the wild white cracks and deep angry recesses
and it explains nothing, not even the tiniest parts
of a childhood I don't remember anymore.

Spinning Them

When the children are released into the waiting arms of the strangers
who have already drank too much
I am, wherever I am, the strange dark woman in the center,
holding them up and spinning them.

They know it's time for bed soon
and when we are pushed into the night,
the children crying in their mother's arms,
right before we had been spinning in our white dresses,
the purity of the moment almost too much for any of us to bear.

Blood Running Out to Sea

You waited twenty years, put your babies away,
watched them swim upstream to spawn with another whose color
you despised. Watched something wild and true wither away
and moved to the Plains to be with a fish locked
in Christ's box. You are locked in too, but not in the same box,
you are in the one that shifted forms moving upstream to die,
though you never thought they'd die together,
not with her still locked in the box, secret and alone.
You thought one day the force of this ocean would crush it,
the blood running out to sea, back into your waiting arms.

Glowing Faintly

The sunflowers painted on garage doors, Diné and Spanish
and English blending into a song downtown and the lights,
the neon lights everywhere, glowing faintly until it's almost like a sound,
music, a tiny humming that you can hear in the night, a million tiny skins
inside the bars, a symphony behind closed doors,
the crisp desert air everything you need before you join them
and let the music drive you down that old, dusty road
it's been meaning to take you on for years.

Arcing Towards the Sun

Wandering through these stores, their strange, wasted
version of us everywhere, I can see how you were once a dancer,
like my mother, how you both still are, your long brown hands arcing
towards the sun. And for him. Whoever he was. And for the days you saw
in a vision once, now faded and gone, like a black and white photograph
you might've picked up as a girl, lost somewhere in the middle
of the dusty city you now call home.

A Thousand Horses Out To Sea

Mama tucked the coffee can between her wrist and hip and walked down Dry Creek Road. Her eyes lined-up, blush and lipstick, her Levi's shorts cut above the thigh. And what it was to see those farmers cutting down wheat, side-glancing mama, barefoot and brown.

-Santee Frazier

Cold and Tired Wind

We moved quickly through the rain soaked streets, and I could feel
your long dark fingers on the back of my seat, in a stranger's car. Those hands
on the small of my back. Once, the heat of you and me reduced
to a few hours in this large, wet city.

We stopped in the street by the market, eating falafel with the other poet,
and you pulled a picture of your dark eyed child out of the pocket
of your worn out jeans, a boy who is now living as you did, without.

When it was time for you to catch a ferry I ran with you, down streets,
past a man begging, a large old drum between his legs, his eyes lighting up at us,
our white heat, asking you what you could possibly be doing with me.

We laughed and I asked you to wait, come back;
it was only to hand you my name in red, and you took it,
the years before stretching in the space between your hand and mine,
our fingers together like angry, delicate flowers
growing in a garden that waits in a secret cave somewhere underground,
where there is just enough wind and sun for a thousand green shoots to grow
and move in the cold and tired wind, a wind now completely gone.

Withering for Months in the Cold

The purple flowers grew up
and around my chairs, those same flowers
that grew everywhere on 66, adding their turbulent beauty
to this place, their delicate green vines withering for months in the cold,
only to be reborn to something I barely understood, my failure
to keep my feet planted anywhere a ghost that haunts this city
when I return with the season, when I return
to place my fingers on those delicate purple flowers and wait
for the revelation that never comes.

The Light of the Television Everywhere

It was a miserable month, a cheap bottle of vodka and the streets, the light
of the television everywhere. I took walks, I can say that, passing huge, opulent
houses into the neighborhood that looked more like mine, that gorgeous boy
with his skin shining in the light and shaved head, asking me where I was from
and where my man was. How beautiful we were on opposite sides of the fence,
our tattoos wrapping around our arms like vines, choking and lovely, eating
the whole world like a snake. I barely got away with a smile, the bird on my arm
taking flight, his words the ones I'll never write.

In That Place That No Longer Exists

I touched you in that place that no longer exists,
in those lost white apartment buildings behind your father's house,
your sad, almost Indian face moving drunkenly towards mine.

I gave you so little, and how you curved into yourself when I left,
the memory of your cold white hands in my black hair almost unbearable,
like something old and dusty, left in the corner of one of those old, abandoned

houses in Idaho Springs where we grew up, doomed to stay, forgotten, fading,
its stuffing moving outward in time, until your father came around
and bulldozed the whole angry, windy, creaking mess down.

The Wonder of the Wonder of It

It's all bright colors and the sounds of things colliding with the earth when you
touch me, or try, speaking of the way your feet might move, the letters you
could write on my skin, my skin, your skin, yellow and glowing in the light,
the wonder of the wonder of the wonder the safety too. What
did your grandmother look like and what did she say, my small head that same
ocean of black, we pull out to sea, dark, lovely, and full of pain, the red-brown
ochre of her skin, something I barely remember, something I know you can't
see anymore, blinded by the sun you move into as you walk into the light.

A Thousand Horses Set Out to Sea

She loved them all, her long hair shimmering porcupine quills,
covering every angel, every boy she set free to run.

It's been awhile, she'd say, since she'd seen the wild horses in the hills,
legs so strong. She'd kiss their long necks in the back of my bronco,

stroking and murmuring in their ears, the echo of their fears
floating to the front as I'd drive and drive.

In the back of her trailer she'd charge forth, fearless and demanding, her fists
clenched and wanting more, the horses transforming into shaking hands.

Sometimes, when I'd look into her eyes, as black and pitiless as my own,
I'd feel like I was watching a thousand horses set out to sea.

At the Edge of Drowning

I've been thinking about her in the bathtub lately,
her tiny brown arms in the middle of the storm;
she's resting, against my flawed brown body
she's so strong, but we could drown
as easily as any child
against any shoulder
taken up against
any arm, and
out of the water,
tiny oceans
full of thunder,
so much
electricity,
motion,
always
at the edge
of drowning.

Crossings in the Night

I destroy
myself, push
all of the borders with a song,
those corridos, those 49's on the edge
of everything beautiful, those crossings in the night
that nobody sees but the ones who are crossing, blind
and waiting for the final vision, the one salvation; mary, yussun—
save the ones who have nothing to lose, nothing to gain.

Fort Peck Girl
~for M.L.S. a.k.a. M.B.

On that night in the bar, she spoke about anger
and I touched my scars as the bodies wound all around us, she and I
only just beginning to measure the distances the exist between people
in bars, between everyone.

She, most beautiful Indian girl I've ever known. Fort Peck girl, body
straight as an arrow in the soil, her mother's initials tattooed on her
back, right beneath the great red wings of the thunderbird stretching
poetically above.

Those wings floated down as I helped her into her dress, yes,
the one she will wear at her altar, at his, at ours, the one we wear
under all of our wings when we love enough to risk bringing
down the first altar, the one that says we must worship

alone.

Wild Blue Glory

I need someone to break me, shake me,
pull me apart. I need violence, blood and sap
running down my long yellow arms,

a tree cracked open by thunder,
branches bent over with love, longing,
rough bark breaking apart like skin.

Once, as a child, I ran through the woods
looking for something:
a tiger lily, elk, my own strange heart.

Oh, the green stink of new roots
like the undead pulling up towards sky.
The primitive blue glory,
the rain, the storm.
The violence of these hands.

Past Both of Us

When I came back home, I walked into the garden
of old tires and parts of cars that no one really wanted,
your man stepping out from behind this jungle, his hands
holding a rag smelling of gasoline, your children behind you
among weeds, their eyes as Aztec as yours, the boys you made blind
with desire now long gone, or having coffee down the road at the Derby.

Either way, now like the dust that your bare feet kicked up,
floating in the wind past both of us.

Knotty Little Prisons

He was blind, and the first boy to ever touch me,
his sister, the terrible thief,
made me sleep in the top bunk with him.

On the bus he would place his hands on my face,
and feel the height of my cheekbones, the slant of my eyes
and he'd offer to take his eye out and laugh. We'd talk bitterly
about escaping our knotty little prisons, the maze of that town
as intricate as any puzzle.

Earlier, she had pulled out her suitcase full of makeup
and we had painted ourselves sick. That same suitcase
that carried the pictures of her father.
Don't you miss him? My mother asked.
No, I have these pictures, she said, and isn't that the same?

Her parents used to make her clean the house everyday, the
things she had to do. God, she was so small.

Later, she married another Skin, and that was strange for me
thinking of her tiny white body in that bed with a body like mine,
dark, and watching her the way I used to, but with lust instead of pity,
the way she used to spit chewing tobacco from her small, shivering pink mouth,
how her brother finally got away, how we both did,
how neither one of us has ever really left home.

Strange Little Bird

She was as beautiful as a strange little bird,
her wasted brown arms closing around her family
as they lifted her from place to place.

She stared back at me with her dark dark eyes
sometimes intense and sometimes dreaming, I used to dance
she'd say, and how old is your mother?

She came across almost 100 years ago
into El Paso, her daughter telling me
that she'd forgotten what tribe she was a long, long time ago.

Tell us about Chango! her family would say
and she'd sour and tell them that they couldn't call him that,
a love so far in the past, he'd become her church,

her eyes closing, her head tilting, a secret smile about her mouth,
the boy who had danced with her, dancing with her,
one of the many who couldn't or wouldn't follow her into the blue.

Carnivorous, Devouring

They were carnivorous
devouring each other without sex
or love, black holes with dark skin
and blond hair, hating the center of themselves,
a terrible beast that dissolved everything in its path and I waited
and prayed with my yellow hands spread wide on the large oak table,
knowing exactly what happens when something like this
sets down long enough to make a storm of its own.

Back in the Storm

I know how to tame this beast, just this one, put its claws away
and wrap my long dark hair around him while we sleep, his breath
the motion at my fire, he's captured it, and it burns brightly
between his two paws, and he stares in wonder at the strange
unquenchable thing he holds, he knows only that it burns that brightly,
at the edge of his ocean, the water coming up, and back in the storm.

THAT SMALL WOODEN BOX

And time moves like a slow rusty train through the desert
of weeds, and the low-riders bounce like teenagers young
and forgiving in her night's dream. She was sleek in a red
dress with red pumps, the boys with slick hair, tight jeans.

-Sheryl Luna

Rescue Me, Rescue Me

I remember she used to tie herself up, beg
for the boys to untie her,
rescue me rescue me she'd say,
her pretty yellow skin shining in the light,
in the forest, for the trees, she made them sing,
every color running their lips along the edge
of her name.

She had them in thrall
she had every boy under her tiny foot,
until daddy came out of the house
and not to play.

Much like the day he ran down the drive,
a semi of anger, silent,
my words dying on my lips as I was flipped
over in front of my friends on the ground, struck
for all of us playing in the street, left to sing into the dirt.

My sister, my mother and her U-Haul
and I, none of us
could ever move fast or far enough.

Ghosts, now. And what,
I ask them, could you possibly want?
There is nothing left.

Waiting For Fire

She was waiting for fire,
her hands resting on her lap, that open field of endless
summer days, green everywhere, daisies burning when
moments before they had been bending in the wind.

She looks up, and his face is nothing like her face,
though they share the same brown skin. And at night,
fingers over fingers over light brown fingers, under the light
of the streetlamp outside herself, the orange glow
filtering in.

When they finish, and she has breath again,
she looks outside, and, seeing herself burning,
the fields on fire, she pulls the curtain aside
to watch the snow cool the burn. How slowly
it falls.

She remembers her grandmother's hands,
the veins, the heat, like tiny animals onto themselves,
folding over and over
making those God's eyes, the yarn, the words
in Chickasaw coming to her then, *daughter,*
she'd say, though she was not, *hold this thread.*
how easily it pulls apart, how easy the final fire.

Other Forests

He's home, and he's waiting for her,
one hand buried deep in his curly brown hair,
the other holding a cigarette, the ash long,
his arm resting on the fading yellow chair.
She's like a fruit, ripe, exploding off the tree
a Cree beauty no man can truly hold, their hands
reaching for a taste of her skin, she must move on,
her daddy taught her well, there are other trees
to cling to, other forests. Her hair so dark, her laughter
wind across the plains, cruel and lonely and irresistible.

Into the Ghosts of Our Ears

The other boy left, the one who sang Diné so sweet on the page, and this boy,
with his car wreck beauty song, the details on the paper a symphony of pain;
taking his chance, diving off the cliff of himself, his hands beautiful brown birds
wanting to alight on my yellow skin; wanting in. He spoke of his mother,
who sang Cherokee into his ear, about his flat face so achingly beautiful,
his voice close to her breath, you can't save her, I thought, but didn't say
because he knew, his hands pausing on the wet brown bar in the middle
of that cold, lit city, all of the poets gone home, both of us waiting
for the words his mother might sing into the ghosts of our ears.

I Fear that My Heart is a Cup

I fear that my heart is cup,
that if I tell that you have drained it,
with your beautiful brown hands,
those same hands that I held up to the sun,
that you will come back,
and with the blackbirds overhead, the birds overhead,
you will drink again, the moment I have filled it,
and leave me with my empty cup,
the birds and my own two eyes black
as the night, as the birds, as my heart overhead.

You Can't Keep Them

You can't keep them unless you tuck tuck tuck
                            them in bed at night
good boy good boy, night night sleep tight
mommy's going to go back to her room and burn
                                 her sweetgrass
the smell of it rich and like the Pendleton and like the hands
that held held held her
                rosary
her eyes closed and praying to the mad mad mad mad
                                maddened
parts of you both.

That Small Wooden Box

Why does it always end up in grass, dirt, stars, where we all go
for release. We will come again and again and again. Your eyes, I hold you,
I fuck you, fuck you, fuck me come in (me) boy and shut the rusty screen
door tight, don't let the cat out, let me hold your mixed blood head

in my mixed blood arms. Look how dirty we've gotten, we're covered in grass,
blood, mine, hers, yours. Perhaps this too will fade, the memories a closet full of
old glass, sky clouding over for days, the way my heart wavers with the wind,
something strange and musical in the air. But no one better open the door,

or we will all get cut, bleed into the night, the grass, the dirt.
Tell me, where is that small wooden box that someone buried long ago,
somewhere in the grass, in the night, lost lost they buried it and died
with the secret; we are the thing it hunts and we will never be found.

Outside My Window at Night, Lovesick

Moving East from my childhood,
I hear her screaming at night,
her sound wild, full of reckless passion.

I wake, strange from sleeping
and look out the window, her body moving
like nothing else, her sound an electric, terrible music.

She and her kind are coming back and I can hear her hunting
outside my window in the terrible darkness, lovesick
the dogs barking a warning she cannot heed.

Jump Over the Line And Join Him

The first one has gone first, the one born of blood and pain,
his ghost making the rounds, his body quick and running
through my sister's house, dissolving, I smudged for him,
and touched the beaded purse he gave me as a child.

The red, the black, the white smooth and terrible under your fingers
count them up with your eyes closed and think like the women he loved,
so many in his childlike arms, crying for them and for his mother,
his hair stiff and black and unforgiving under their fingers.

The things he said were probably unforgivable
but once over the cliff you have to forgive,
you cannot hold on, you must close your eyes and jump
over the line and join him in the big black space of your very own heart.

Until the Sun Rises

She is the woman with the crown of thorns around her neck, pull, pull, lead her, watch her bleed for you, the red running down, she will be lead in the desert for four days and she will pray with her own blood and will ask for nothing in return but a moment inside your hot brown hands, yes, the same ones that pray around her neck. God, you have to tell me that you know what you are doing because I am the one that watches and waits, I hold the thorns that she has left in my hand, I close my fist, I bleed, I wait for a fist to grow inside her, I wait for the desert to pull back, for the ceremony with pollen to finally make her a woman, so she can take the desert inside her and bring forth the wide, white, blinding sheets of rain, the kind that takes everything into the forces we cannot control, the ones far outside of his hands, the desert and me and into the moment of change, the moment we will all look East, to be born and born and born again.

Long Aching Body in the Desert

I remember her curly dark blonde hair, her bruises, her look of love
that thing that blossoms inside you like whiskey, like pain
like the most beautiful sunset you've ever seen, the one
with the oranges, the yellows, the reds, his fist
on her face.

They laughed, and told her yes
I'm sure he's fucking someone else
and she said are you sure are you sure
and they said no.

I was there, invisible,
thinking of him, his long brown hands,
his Indian mother who surely spoke Spanish,
her long aching body in the desert, searching
for an answer, finding
a white face just like the ones in front of this woman,
her son's lover, her hands so deeply calloused from work,
they looked like wounds.

And him, her love, his hard
black Government Issue glasses
something he brought out only
when wanting to see better;
incoming traffic, wide silver doors leading to light, her face,
just before the fall of his own hands. Otherwise,
just another strange object his fingers would brush past
in the pockets of his old black jeans, the holes
a doorway to a mother he'd never known,
his father a hard white stone.

All of the Sighs Have Gone

I've always loved the thunderstorms,
clean, violent, like a lover's hand. The kind that takes you
and it's all thunder and noise and wet
windows, the glass shaking like it might break,
your head back on the pillow, your hands in his black, black hair.

After, when the sun comes
out, and all of the sighs have gone,
outside there is a newness, and no matter
how many times you've seen this come and go,
it's new, the Huisache Dulce wild and wet
and yellow, it's brush pushing up into the sky,
like it's working hard to reach the sun,
to be burned out of existence,
like a light, in the night, that must go out.

Long, Yellow and Stretching Lazily

I'm bad, I'll win. With my red lipstick and my red lights,
like lanterns in the night, leading the way to whatever
I desire. I will take all of them for myself, a glutton, a shapeshifter,
something that stops over in the night, and wakes up into a different
body. Long, yellow and stretching lazily like a wolf in the mid-afternoon sun,
I want to be the hunter, I want to be the gun.

Folding Over and Over and Over

Blindfold me, lead me into your desert, you know
how I like sex in the dark,
dark, small, unknown parts of your dark dark hands.

Here it is again, the dust, the heat, the red, red
parts of us both, I breathe you in, you take me down,
apart. I am like an old blue car in your hands.

The Virgin de Guadalupe hangs in the sky,
she turns her head, not because it is a sin,
but because she knows me,
knows how the desert takes, and does not return,
her dust folding over and over and over,
a wild, lonely wind that no one hears,
a clock that has not even begun to tick,
sand stuck between twelve and one.

How Big and Cruel the Ocean

It's like the man said; it's a doorway that opens straight into the ocean, a nothingness, a knife, the blade that you took to yourself to cut the parts of your grief away, the big black curls sitting at your feet. I imagine you staring into the mirror of his eyes, the black of them behind those bars all of those miles and miles across the desert away, the wind blowing like the sound of a train at midnight. Lonely and tidal. Fall, fall in, sink into this ocean, think of his prayers of forgiveness and hate me for my big, red blood instead. Close, close your eyes boy let the cold seep in, the knife in your heart twisting and twisting in the kind of pain that nothing can spirit away. Your lips against my hair in the dark, how you said you wanted to bundle it up in your hands. . . how small your voice was, how large his, how strong my hands, how big and cruel this ocean.

High Winds Over Mountains

Stomp, stomp, move around that fire girl, quick, quick, in time, with the jingles around your ankles, don't lose that song. Don't look to the side to see if he's singing, if he's still there. He's still there. Think about your mother, how she missed this fire, this heat, how her mother's eyes were closed by her own hand, the shot that rang out, the sound of your mother wailing downstairs like an animal. You were six but you still remember the high winds over mountains sound of her pain. You must keep the beat, or this fire will go out, the one laying softly in the candle, the one she lit for prayers, her eyes closed, thinking only of you and your soft, small yellow arms deep inside your mother's deep inside hers, like a secret no one has to keep. Keep time, remember that your father read to you as a child, that was his song, the thing in-between the fists and the drink and calling your mother a whore. You must remember that he is there too, that he is in that fire with your grandmother and wants you to dance. They all want you dance, the living and the dead and the ones living as if they were dead, the huffers, the drinkers, the ones who will cause women to wail for them soon. You have to dance for them, you have to sing for them, in their silence is a great cat moving through the silver of the night, she steals into the fire, she brings everything back.

Receding Like the Wilderness in the Night

Under the stars, the smell of the desert everywhere, L leans over and talks about Peyote and S about the Stomp, and we are all wide open and looking up and it is beautiful for a moment, my eyes meeting S's eyes, we roll off into the distance, me sitting on the hood of the sliver, silver car in my green, green dress, shimmering with the heat that has already left this place. Don't think, don't think about the next day, the wandering through the desert, the children screaming in your ear, the watching of the bodies melt, the things you have to know about men. This is when the desert does not bloom, it is when it cuts you open and reveals a wound that cannot heal, the one that is cut precisely in the shape and shadow of your father. His hands reach out in the dark, they implore for forgiveness, and then they withdraw, like the shadow that they finally are, moving slowly across the red desert floor, receding like the wilderness and into the night.

Smoke Billowing

Walking alone in this cold Chicago night,
my worn red heels echoing in these wild dusty streets,
the taquerias glowing green & white, the smell of cooking meat everywhere,
I think of you and smoke, my hands moving like anxious children in the dark.

A man with a long black mustache passes,
his wide brown face broken and sad and full of this large white city,
Ah Senorita . . . he sighs.

Yes, I am the woman we laughed about,
the tall, the yellow, angry dark haired woman,
I am full of your betrayal,
my face plastered on every window, every ancient black door,
I'm selling mangos, horchata, sex, phone cards;
just another lonely Indian, posing as everything else,
searching for fire, smoke billowing out of me like a factory.

The Slant and Dark

Look at her, staring at him, at his body,
moving as restlessly as a school of fish.

How alike our faces are;
the slant and dark of our eyes.
The hair that consumes all light,
collapsing in on itself like a dying star.

In the cornfields, I watched my heart,
light years from my body, and it was beautiful
and distant as the powwow music floating from the car.

Her eyes close. My heart comes near, the fields sway
in the wind, in the night. The music comes into us,
and we move in the rapidly receding light, the darkness
coming on; all of the boys we have ever loved, one boy,
one dark thing, a wild, ubiquitous field swaying in the night.

Safety Dream

And you, and you, with your sleepy child bride on the couch,
her small blonde head resting near your arm
you think of my darkness,
the way my Indian hair filled the hollow of your neck,
my moans, my cries . . . my cries . . . inside me
grandmother closes her eyes as you enter, saying
the only way this works for me is to forget.
Yes, forget, forget, forget your strange whisper that you loved me,
quiet now, go to sleep, join her world on the couch. That safety dream,
the one, the only one, I never knew.

The Way Your Mouth

The pulling up of the sock
the breath, the sex of it
your listless face, everything
is strange in this place,
the cold, the snow, once
you whispered it, you won't let go
my arms are too weak
and I'm such a funny girl, the joke,
the cold, I'm looking out the window
at night, the cars roll by, one of them
is yours.

You stare out your window
into mine, the cigarettes in the dark, the music
of this thing, the color of your skin, mine,
hers. The words on the page are monsters,
they eat, the way your mouth consumes mine.

Quiet now, quiet,
I am already inside of you
and you are burning,
shovel, shovel the coal,
bury me deep in your furnace
or I may rise up, a phoenix, and burn us all.

I Made Love to an Empty House

I made love to an empty house
a ghost ship; I am the lighthouse,
your dirty brown secret your light
smashed, broken into, vandalized.

Glass is everywhere, no more light
out to sea leading you towards shore.

Lost, lost, like a child crying in the night
holding your arms up and screaming
your white mouth against my dark breast

You drown, you drown
lost out to sea your anger a weight
pulling you down.

And Finally

And finally, you've gone, though by force and not choice, your threats turning out to be nothing. The students you've fucked, their round empty faces, move on without really caring. Their stories, all copies, their white empty pages, all glitter with traces cocaine. They tell me your secrets, the parties, the anger, and laugh behind mocking white fingers. Your colleagues, all strangers, move on and don't get it, with concepts of artist resounding. Your tiny ex-wife, the one who you ran from, sits staring at walls in the city. Her strange little heart, her stories of silence, rot on the vine of your making. Your emails, your texts, your paranoid lies, all sit in a databank somewhere. And all through the night, the peace of your going unfolds like a dark woven blanket. Something my grandmother never could teach me, her hands like a strange copper bracelet. What the students don't know, and the colleagues can't reach, is the man that I knew in our office. The dancing performer with first person, third, each view-point a thrust with a smile. You honking your horn when you knew that you loved me, your white freckled hands on my thigh. Your telling of neighbors who now you've deleted of what you thought was my brilliance. Your strange groaning sighs and whispers of love that I keep even though you deleted. And though there were times when I knew it was selfish, your hours and hours with students. The fact that you never, no matter what happened, picked up the bottle again. Unlike my father who you truly resemble, and who I can love now through you. And I know that you're ruined, will rot in a city, your words dying quick on the vine. But I'll always remember the pages I read, the wow of iambic pentameter. And I know that you'll sit, sucking smoke after smoke, thinking of me and your father. Your hands growing old, your face in the mirror, the shame that you feel every day. But I'll keep who you were, your vulnerable smile, for you and for me and for them. The days will float by, the memories haunting, the green growing fast on the vine. The rain and the sun and the leaves always falling, your heart in my heart in the line.

Light Over the Grass

More fireflies. And after you've left me;
forever this time. That cold, blue mountain has finally taken you,
the way that I never could; your body,
that lanky brown body I loved so much, trapped in ice,
forever pure and still and smelling of sweetgrass.
Oh M, Mark, my M, my light, my wound, my muse, my heart,
you are the light dancing over the grass . . . my God, where you have finally
gone?

Acknowledgments

"As Distant as a Planet," *Hysteria*, forthcoming.

"Wild Blue Glory," *Hysteria*, forthcoming.

"Ghosts Floating on the Flat White Bed," *Rabbit and Rose*, 2015.

"Around My Neck," *About Place*, 2015.

"That Small Wooden Box" *Tin Cannon*, 2015.

"Long, Yellow and Stretching Lazily" *Tin Cannon*, 2015.

"On North Beach" *Toe Good Poetry*, 2013.

"Faces Toward the light" *Mas Tequila Review,* 2013.

"Change Form Behind Me" *Mas Tequila Review,* 2013.

"He Brought Me Down" *As, Us,* 2013.

"Fists Clenched, Holding" *As, Us,* 2013.

"Dusty Redemption" *Yellow Medicine Review*, 2013.

"Receding Like the Wilderness in the Night" *Cimarron Review*, 2013.

"Smoke Billowing" *Cimarron Review*, 2013.

"At the Edge of Drowning" *The Cape Rock*, 2012.

"Until the Sun Rises" *Drunken Boat*, 2011.

Erika T. Wurth's novel, *Crazy Horse's Girlfriend*, was published by Curbside Splendor. Her first collection of poetry, *Indian Trains*, was published by The University of New Mexico's West End Press. A writer of both fiction and poetry, she teaches creative writing at Western Illinois University and has been a guest writer at the Institute of American Indian Arts. Her work has appeared or is forthcoming in numerous journals, such as *Boulevard, Drunken Boat*, and *South Dakota Review*. She is represented by Peter Steinberg. She is Apache/Chickasaw/Cherokee and was raised outside of Denver.

CPSIA information can be obtained
at www.ICGtesting.com
Printed in the USA
LVOW05s1226020117

519400LV00008B/931/P

9 780997 251739